THE FLAVOR OF THE OTHER

CLARA BURGHELEA

Nevenka,
for my friend
the golden fish
Slavic &
of the USA!

DOS MADRES
2020

LOVE,
Christine

DOS MADRES PRESS INC.
P.O.Box 294, Loveland, Ohio 45140
www.dosmadres.com editor@dosmadres.com

Dos Madres is dedicated to the belief that the small press is essential to the vitality of contemporary literature as a carrier of the new voice, as well as the older, sometimes forgotten voices of the past. And in an ever more virtual world, to the creation of fine books pleasing to the eye and hand.

Dos Madres is named in honor of Vera Murphy and Libbie Hughes, the "Dos Madres" whose contributions have made this press possible.

Dos Madres Press, Inc. is an Ohio Not For Profit Corporation and a 501 (c) (3) qualified public charity. Contributions are tax deductible.

Executive Editor: Robert J. Murphy

Illustration & Book Design: Elizabeth H. Murphy
www.illusionstudios.net

Typeset in Adobe Garamond Pro & Constantia
ISBN 978-1-948017-64-0
Library of Congress Control Number: 2019952368

First Edition

Published by Dos Madres Press, Inc.

ACKNOWLEDGEMENTS

This work would not have been possible without the support of my beehive: Lydia Renfro, Michelle Bermudez, Juan Chemes, Andreea Mottram, Raluca Marinescu, Dana Vasiloiu, Jill Massino. Thank you for the reading hours and your caring hearts. You kept me on my toes and wishing to better myself. I am especially indebted to my Adelphi professors Igor Webb, Judith Baumel, Martha Cooley, Katherine Hill, Kermit Frazer, and Michael Matto who were supportive of my career goals and worked actively to provide me with the protected academic time to pursue those goals.

I am grateful to all of those with whom I had the pleasure to work during my Creative Writing program at Adelphi University and other related projects: Jon, Matt, Sarah, Anna, Choya, Jordan, MJ, Chris, Dani, Iris, Rachel, Kelsi, Krista, Robin. Grateful to Codruța, Edvin, my Bridges family, my international friends. I am lucky to have had the support of my New York family- Neculai and Claresa, and my Rochester family- Val, Dana and Alexandra.

I would especially like to thank poet Jacqueline Jones LaMon. As my professor and mentor, she has taught me more than I could ever give her credit for here. She has shown me, by personal example, what a good poet, educator and human being should be.

I would like to thank my publisher, Robert Murphy, from Dos Madres Press, whose elegance and patience have guided me through the process of curating my collection.

I couldn't have written these poems without the inspiration of these wonderful poets: Kimberly Grey, Kristina Marie Darling, Dorianne Laux, Kim Addonizio, Jack Gilbert, Rachel McKibbens, Airea D Matthews, Kaveh

Akbar, Charif Shanahan, Maggie Smith, Leila Chatti, Rosa Alcalá, Adélia Prado, Ştefan Manasia, Nina Cassian, Dan Coman, Adrianne Rich, Sharon Olds, and many others.

Nobody has been more important to me in the pursuit of this project than the members of my family. I would like to thank my father, my two grandmothers, my brother, my in-laws, whose love, guidance and support are with me in whatever I pursue. My heart will always be with my beloved mother. I miss you every blinking moment!

Most importantly, I wish to thank my loving and supportive husband, Iulian, and my two wonderful children, Saşa and Mihnea, who provide unending inspiration. I love you desperately!

Grateful acknowledgement is made to the editors of the following journals, in which versions of these poems originally appeared:

As Above So Below: 'Daughterhood'
Barzakh: 'Aubade'
Better Than Starbucks: 'Habitation'
Burning House Press: 'Inadequacies'
Dodging the Rain: 'Memory', 'My Amputations'
Fishbowl Press: 'Skin is one way of knowing'
Harana Poetry: 'Sandpaper'
Havik Anthology: 'The Body's Questions', 'Clara and Cătălin'
Here: A Poetry Journal: 'First Time: Orange'/*Portocale*
Isacoustic Volume Fourth: 'How to Lose a Self in a Few Steps'
K'in Magazine: 'A Stranger's Doing'
LEVITATE: 'The View from Here'
Mockingheart Review: 'Migratory'
Multimedia Poetry and Art Journal: 'A Certain Swirl'
Peach Velvet Magazine: 'Missing is'

Poetry Breakfast: 'Resilience'
Poetry Leaves: 'Motherhood'
Poetry Magazine: 'The body is the most dangerous place to be'
Porter Gulch Review: 'Homemade Love', 'Displacement'
Recenter Press: 'A Kind of Burning'
The Bitchin Kitsch: 'The pain, the evil and the brevity of summer days'/'Excavation'
The Blue Nib: 'To this day', 'Process of Detachment'
The Citron Review: 'Mirage'
The Friday Influence: 'The Self as Introduction'
The Ideate Review: 'The Want that Wants to Be Wanted'
The Pangolin Review: 'Self-exile', 'Hymn to Life'
The Wild Word: 'Things My Mother Brought to Life'
Toe Good: 'A Taxonomy of Smells'
Toasted Cheese: 'The Strings of Demi-Gods'
Vita Brevis Literature: 'Thieves'
***Where Are You From? Anthology*:** 'Distilled Light'
Witches: 'Keeping Things Whole'
Yes Poetry: 'Oversimplified'

To my lovelies: Iulian, Sașa and Mihnea

THE FLAVOR OF THE OTHER

Table of Contents

The stiff wind left
in their mouths, a strange taste
of bile, of mint, and of basil
My friend, where is she—tell me—
where is your bitter girl?'

Federico García Lorca

A Taxonomy of Senses

(after Joshua Bennet)

As grass and filthy hands. As burnt matches.
As hard-boiled eggs dyed in onion skins on Good Friday.
As a father's rage. As newly born flesh.
As fish grease in a cold house. As caged grief.
As the pain of the one-legged woman on the R Train.
As a father's tireless gaze.
As my mother's supple ghost.
As warm bread sold on ration card -never enough.
As a half-bird living in a flight of humans.
As chants nestled inside the brain.
As a wise son calling his mother a feline.
As ink on the tips of fingers. As pain cracks.
As flirting with a tall stranger.
As a tooth falling into the mother's palm.
As a little brother choking on cherries.
As if life took a halt.
As surviving this flesh. As reading "loss" in a poem.
As a lover's shadow. As false teeth in a dirty glass.
As god built inside little walls. As me.

Portocale

(RM.VALCEA, ROMANIA, 1985)

Mother comes back in the morning, after a night of queuing. Her treasures lay on the kitchen table: four oranges, two rolls of soft toilet paper, a half-melted bar of Chinese chocolate. I touch the fruit and put my nose to it. The smell tickles the roof of my mouth. Mother smiles and starts peeling. Her agile long fingers, soaked with juice, run across the white flesh of the fruit. The grainy rind coils on her lap like a baby snakeskin. *Mamaia* stares over her thick rims while her hands keep up the purring sound of knitting socks. The orange blooms into fleshy petals on the plate, and all three of us gaze at its layered pulp. Eyes half closed, we taste the twinned heart of the fruit. Outside the window, happy laundry dances across a green line. In my hand, chocolate melts like love.

Thieves

In the belly of summer
heat peels off like onion skin,
the burning ribcage of the day
cracks open and more sweltering air spills out.
Five of us sit on the pavement,
exchanging first-class stamps.
Guinea Bissau is the much-craved winner.
We spend days
begging for coins from our parents
to buy more envelopes,
hearts pounding
as we open them.

The stamps are tiny, too delicate for sticky fingers.
Histories of nations lie within the perforated edges
and teach us to practice vigilance.
We squint to capture the details.
'Look, a hair stuck to every Guinea Bissau!'
Only two of us found the golden stamps
and proudly keep our books open
for sighs and envious gazes.
Wildly colored mushrooms
reveal their flashy caps
to curious eyes
that dilate in fascination.
All lavish stamps are framed
by a golden rim.

The rest of us look
at our useless Romanian stamps
and try to swap them for Russian ones
whose rectangular shapes work better
in our albums. No value whatsoever.

When all negotiation closes
we are reminded of our hungry stomachs.
Without much planning
but performing a well-known routine
we head for the marketplace.

Piles of egg-shaped striped
watermelons ripen in the quiet sun.
Behind them, tired farmers
rest their numb limbs
on colorful rugs, hats over
eyes, calloused palms on chests.
Two of us keep a lookout
wandering, hands in pockets
no worry in the world.
The other three tiptoe
and circle the dusty fruit.
They stop to listen to the wheezing
breath of the farmer,
punctured by coughing spells.
When the voice of a mother
calling her son,
breaks the silence,
they grab the prey and run laughing.
The farmer jumps to his feet,
confused, alarmed.

Inside our apartment building,
under the staircase,
we crack the watermelon open
and thrust our teeth
into its pink flesh.
Juice dripping down chins and elbows,
we spit seeds at each other,
precious ammunition
that ends up under our tacky feet.
A morsel of life eaten.
And time, the unaware thief.

Woundology

Bad girls are made to kneel on walnut shells,
get earrings taken out of their pink ears,
see their mom bend to punchable noise.
A rash of grief sheening on her worn skin.
They are told to apologize for their nasal voice,
the savage hair, the temper, the awakenings.
Beyond the window, their flesh and hunger
go hand in hand. Their gait, a stemmed whisper.
They make private constellations out of scars.
Thin limbs breathing secret warmth into book covers.
The worlds set in their hearts thunder
a thousand storms, yet no whirlwind
sweeps them away from the two-room flat
where they shrink into themselves. Old souls.

Clara and Cătălin

spring children,
born 14 months apart
same pair of knitted eyebrows,
mother wound in both chests.

We, sharing
the heartbreaking abundance
of little things- oranges for Christmas,

Chinese chocolate
at Easter.
In between, homemade pies,
flour and sugar on food coupons.

We, radio kids,
never owned a cassette player,
yet knew how to rewind
using a pencil.

We, bruised knees,
kings of cherry trees
and smuggled bubble gum,
sold at the street corner.

We, dreaming in color,
washed bottles and jars
to sell for coins to sell
for stamps to sell for movie tickets.

We, eating pumpkin seeds
on the dusty pavement,
chanting names
of hard-shelled American heroes:

Darth Vader, before he had a life,
Laurel and Hardy,
always in black and white,
John Wayne,
making a Western frown.

We, a locket's parted
half-hearts
living without having survived.
This is love the way we know it.

Skin is one way of knowing

the ripeness of the peach
before sinking teeth into flesh,
the sidewalk melting

under the weight of the sun,
rain, before April becomes May,
kisses goodbye, kisses hello,

trees fumbling to pluck the sky,
the open body to be a noun
before blooming into a verb,

how to harvest fresh water from fog,
to appease mother wound,
one step closer to sanity.

Every girl needs help to climb a tree,
touch, a better way of explaining.

Holding

My mother, back from the night shift,
bones cracking, hair infused with lab salts.
'For lunch, eggplant salad on rye bread.'
Lithe fingers on my face, clock hands
on the wall, measuring softness. Inside the palm,
blisters map the motherland. I follow them
with my finger looking for stories.
Through the open window, the sun's yellow tongue runs
over every block of flats, chasing the day.

The Self as Introduction

No wound loathes its scar,
yet craves the radiant absence.

God's laughter punctures
the arch of the sky

every new dawn,
eyes bandaged with light.

What fell from your lips
came to nest into my mouth

the thieving of the heart,
an unpremeditated entry.

The gap on the page,
a muttering under a kiss.

Before the perfect word,
a rustling of the tongue.

Things My Mother Brought to Life

In the closet, among linen,
four green bananas to ripen.
Sometimes, a bar of apple soap,
for doctor visits, never to be used,
its smell tingling our noses.

In the kitchen cupboard,
on the highest shelf, out of reach,
a packet of real coffee,
the silhouette of a red fez boy.
To be traded, upon need.

Honey, the coupon is on the fridge.
Buy bread. Don't lose it again.
A mother's handwriting
is always arched and slender
like a spring day.

I slip the key string around my neck.
Mother crocheted it while waiting
in line for milk. Instead, four oranges.
'Do we save them for Christmas?'
Mother's back cracked like an old bed.

In the street, linden trees are in bloom.
We pick their flower and dry it on
the little balcony. *For sore throat*
and finding your way back.
Their pollen numbs all heartbeat.

Mirage

The day was here
and then it was not.
It could be never more
or less than that-
a chrysalis of promise.

In the realm of lost items,
where earrings, buttons, coins,
chances, words, gazes
cluster like beads,
tongues wait to be awoken.

Time's swiftness lay
in the small details of our skin,
innocuous in their layers,
fragrant when tasted,
pecks of light on its geography.

In the unbridgeable gulf
between before and after,
we were inside,
love swishing in our mouths.
I have kept everything you shed.

My Amputations

You shall not argue, bargain or disobey.
You shall be a good daughter,
make a fine wife one day
and breed like an Orthodox woman.

You shall not want, dare or speak up.
You shall rub floors and backs,
do laundry and favors,
stay home and low.

You shall not have fun, pleasure or dreams.
You shall work long hours,
smile, bow your head,
cook lavish meals and speak softly.

You shall abound in the good work of others.

Amen.

An Afterthought

I think you're safe now.
I've raised a son in your absence,
my roots have turned white
and there is a continent between us.
I still bear you, if not in my flesh,
both old and new, then in the presence
that animates this flesh, your body I washed,
the long bedridden days, our changing of cells.

I've needed words to hang on to you,
fixing the unspoken and the grief
leaping like cracks in the pavement.
I was a fool. Words do not heal.
They plaster the holes and clear space
on a page. At times, pretentiously.
It's been a decade of bargaining
and eluding to call your name.
Now, it is time to let you go, mother.

Lost in Translations

When I plunge into the water, velcro lungs hum
and the island quivers all the way to Etna. Three years
of gentle slumber later, the volcano coughs fistfuls of ash
that glide into the roasting air down Valle del Bove, past
pine trees and orange groves, all the way to the kind shores
of Taormina. I rise above the emerald foam, the sun's heavy
mouth sucks me dry, skin wrinkled like crepe paper. Above the hills,
evening arranges itself under the quiet Sicilian dust, the clarity
of the twilight melting away the heat. The 8 pm Enna Alta
bus is kindly late. The *biggleto* lady frowns, beady sweat rimming
her hairline: *1,2 € por favore*. Stepping in/out of the languages
requires a shedding of the tongue, a death of the bird in the throat.
The red-eyed bulb of the ticket booth scorches its plume.

The body is the most dangerous place to be

2 pm is a treacherous hour,
it ushers into the day,
a smile sinking into a chest.
It can be all lemonade and chat,
or silently cutting so much of you
out of myself, it numbs the fingertips.
The air stung with slumber,
heat, a thin grime on the skin.
The hive of the world
pummeling the absence,
no cell safe from its echo.

A Kind of Burning

As children, mother fed us grapes
and fresh bread before going to school.
My brother's stomach always rumbled
in discord. Recess found us biting our nails,
chasing the sun through the open window.

At noon, keys around our necks,
we dragged our feet to the seventh floor.
Our two-room apartment
greeted us cold and dark.
No electricity after 7 pm.

We sneaked up every day after class
to play elastics with Larisa.
Her mother made sour cherry jam
and we ate it warm from the pot,
laughing at each other's dark teeth.

Grandmother slapped me
for eating at the house of my gypsy friend:
Do you wanna steal like her kind
when you grow up?
She never scolded my brother. I was his keeper.

One day, I kissed Larisa on the mouth
and tasted the tart lips, green eyes piercing my skin.
My brother grinned and pulled my ponytails.
A male admonition. At night, I laid still,
the smell of her hair numbing my body.

Motherhood

My son is trying to sleep,
lamp on, frowned eyes.
A constellation of
beauty marks peppers
the nook of the neck,
the underside of his cheek.
Nothing bad can happen,
there are no monsters.
The lie flies off my lips
and hits the starry ceiling.
Some heavy bird.
This sheerness to his skin
I want to shield. Gut wrenching.
Midmorning, I find him
crawled at my feet,
my own hands turned
into numb fists.
We had both succumbed
to all nightly creatures.
French toast for my brave boy?
A hum from the lowest place of my body.

The dirty-dish poem

Forenoon is slumber,
a Walton Ford kind of day,
all inner beasts tenderly resting

velvet paws and ivory beaks.
The room breathes softly,
blue veins mapping the walls,

all drawers, acutely quiet.
In the sink, plates and cutlery
still bearing the imprints

of your familiar skin. Expectant.
Against the roof of my mouth,
various kinds of self-denial.

In a sense, this is merely preparation
for the narrative of days to come.

Resilience

Grief has a sheen to it.
I close my eyes and think silver,
teeth of a zipper that won't close.
Late, at night, it begs me

to consider its hinges,
long shadow running tongue
over the flimsy details of us,
bones chomping on absence.

I wet a finger with my tongue,
unpack the heart anew,
my face, your face,
we bruise against each other.

At dawn, the scab I keep picking,
pink as a cat's ear, grows more skin.

Homemade Love

First, pick the ripe cherries,
the ones grandpa calls coeur de pigeon,
plump and mushy fleshed,
making your mouth water.
Make sure you hang around your ears
the first two pairs stemmed together.
Never eat those. Grandpa says
the tree will go barren and lose all flower.
You will keep the habit throughout the years,
even when buying cherries,
long after the cheery tree
at the north end of the garden
was cut down, turned into a dry stump,
and your grandfather's voice
becomes some blurred memory.

Then, you drink a shot of vișinată
on his name day, to honor his favorite habit
and spite your brother. He will never bring that up.
Except when you break your arm
and tears stream down your muddy face, yet you don't cry,
but he can smell fear, and start telling stupid things like:
"And remember that time when you…and I….and then grandpa…"
Brother love is tangy and broken heart is small craft,
the span of a man's arms.

At last, dip the bitten cherry into vișinată,
put it between your lips, let it burn,
then bottoms up,
fruity smell stuck into your nose
for decades to come.

Self-exile

Aside from the silence of a woman's absence
and the intimate terrain of grief,
what causes migration in the body?

Space to be wrong.
Space to be small.
Space to be vulnerable.

Turning invisible under the gaze of the other,
unaccounted for and unsung,
being born the wrong kind of animal.

My mental room is full of interruptions.
By slow degrees, I just happened to have died
a couple of times before geography took hold of me
and I started anew.

Drawing my weight against the resistance
of unknown waters,
you, this other I have met at the end of the world,
are an object lesson to learn
before I swim into my skin again.

A Certain Swirl

This is how you survive childhood:
you disappear. Wear ugly macramé
thin-soled flat shoes. Your grandma
crocheted them and by the time she
finished the hitchings, cotton turned
dirty white. At noon, you eat your slice
of sugared bread, an army of coveting
flies in the stale air. You read in bed,
on the floor, under blankets. There is
no place that does not hold you. Except
for your father's gaze. Some murky green
that reeks of cognac. You grow up sniffing
it on all men you date. At times, you hate it.
Mostly, you crave it. In the coffee-soaked
ladyfingers your son carefully places
on the tiramisu plate, in your coffee mug,
in the scented Ikea candle. Your first memory
counts, the one nestling in your blood,
your mother says. Sheets snapping dry
on the clothesline, your shadows folding
starched pillowcases and broken promises.
The windshield wipers of your parents'
1300 Dacia sharply measuring heartbeats
like a metronome. The three of you ride
on even days, never on odd ones. Next
to you, grandma prunes a basket of green
beans, small glasses on her aquiline nose.
Heads go on snapping, their purr soothing
your churning stomachs. Outside the window,
a white June is blooming. You ride face pressed

against the window. A flush from the deepest
thicket of the body, then a burr in the throat.
When you get off at the fish market, the back
of your handmade little skirt sticks to your skin
and all of sudden, faces turn to you. Below
words, mouths taste of rumbling adulthood.
Lurking shame comes with glittering eyes
and the stain grows the size of the Black Sea.
A train whistles in the distance, your thoughts,
shuffling cards. Above the fish stench, a vegan sky.

First Night in New York

In the street, cold dogs with curly tails
of unfamiliar elegance
warm up to quiet pedestrians,
indifferent to their timid eyes.

A season of birdsong
explodes from the tall trees
and the dogs prick their ears,
looking up into the fluted air.

The foreign, thawing bodies
brush up against one another,
spells of cellophane,
fueling the city's motions.

On my window ledge,
a cardinal's red body
looks me in the eye,
uncertain of my pluck.

Behind me, the silence
of my hotel room reads like
an indictment. On TV,
Ava Gardner is lost in Singapore.

Inadequacies

Scarred, thin skin hiding
inside loose T-shirt,
the barren jasmine

softly coiled up
the purple blind's string,
chipped, blue mug burning

my lips seeking yours.
Foreign blood flooding
the room, no way out,

your gaze nowhere to
be found. The leaving
leaves. Pain comes in waves.

Unstructured lean hours
quicken upon touch.

Missing is

an almond tinge
at the corner of your lips
every time I smile,

a nest of mice
gnawing at your bones
dreaming up my flesh,

the oblivious sound of birds
winging behind
your eye windows,

the floating debris of the day
peeling off
over a glass of red wine,

your light purple shirt
before it started missing
buttons,

the whir of days,
light as a whisper,
on your fat cheek,

knowing you can make a home
out of a human being,
yet never stay,

your silences
that hemmed the dawn
and I took shelter in

unspoken words
as if they were
whetstones of sorrow,

like wearing a suit of flesh,
uncomfortable
into your own skin.

Daughterhood

When the MGM lion roars,
memory blisters. The body snaps
like a zipper stuck on its slide.
Inside the little communist theater,
a mother's hand is taffy love.
Touching is charting the flesh,
a warming of the face when fingers
know its fabric. Under the Brooklyn Bridge,
this aliveness of summer not large enough
to fill the pocket of longing.

Aubade

I want to punch the time clocks
with fists of air,
polish my anger
like a blade,
so one morning it will cut
to the core of it
and hands will know purpose.

The fleeting stance of love
lingers still in small, barred places,
unreached by the long itchy hands
that tick and tock,
unhindered,
until I sink back into silence
and am reminded it is gone.

Oversimplified

The room, like a womb. Everything pulses-
the budding jasmine on the window sill,
the January gust through the laced curtains,
the flickering flame of the Ikea berry candle.
Inside my body, stones. Mute like wide terrain.
Your palm, I imagine, wise and cushioned,
reaches through my face, my habits,
across tissues and foul blood,
looking for purpose.
My heart stumbles over harsh syllables.
The stones start flaring into huge bleached space
where I can coil like wounded snake
and hide till something learns to shift anew.

Migratory

Why should the exiled go back?
Even if there is a country, a heart,
a spring to find awaiting.
The mother tongue is tissue-borne,
a place of inwardness
and smoldering fire.
Yet, the path back seems barely findable,
no crumbles, no flags, no undersongs.
Here, winter still claims dominion,
and no crickets shrill in the grass,
yet freedom is an idiom built in flesh
and you grow on it until your skin ripples.
Meanwhile, you turn, measure up
the sky sliding away like an old Egyptian boat
and wear your body of choices. Inside-out.

How to Lose a Self In a Few Steps

First, you read until pairs of invisible eyes
grow under your skin, eating at the paper-
the slip on which you become someone's wife,
then the birth certificate
that spells your daughter's name.
Each time, white birds burst out
of your chest.
The eyes bleed a little,
you have no idea why your skin breaks out.

Branches snap, trees spit out leafy hearts,
easy summers thicken by year.
Here is some rose water to sprinkle
over your thinning sanity.
One day, mother love turns into a wound
the size of a missing breast,
a vicious broth of bone meat and brain failure.
The eyes under the skin close one by one,
failing windows of hearable hum.

Bargaining is nursing your baby boy
while dreaming of your mother's morphine.
Get away from me, come closer,
you say to the man
who knows every here and there in you.

Pain is as pain does. Blind eyes
feel the edges of you that now slip
into unfamiliar geography.
Remember to lose your wedding band,

your true colors, mostly, your liquid mind.
Get a tattoo right above the left wrist
still able to slit it without ruining the pretty letters.
The bearded artist slips his hand between your legs.

Out in the world,
you scatter papers from your desk,
and pulse inside words, books, poems.
You can feel your skin prickling,
surging with ink blood.
The pen voraciously bites at the paper:
I am thinking of you. One day,
you'll visit your own grave and say: passion did it.

Exile

is the way our bodies thaw
against others and dream
of growing new roots,
while still craving
the humming of the bird,
the touch of the wing,
the joy of floating.
Against the same clear skies.

Sandpaper

I don't want to give up longing,
these tines of invisible fork
that puncture the lungs.
Smells like acacias in bloom,
and soap bars in between starched sheets.
Tastes like uneasiness, the way
the stomach churns and pounds
like a trapped animal.
Longing is a rusty old grater
that granulates pain.
It hollows me like a husk,
metal teeth biting at the flesh.
I never bleed though.
I write in ink bursts,
then run fallow for a while.
Small poems jammed together,
bitter-pitted and muffled,
sitting on my chest,
trying to press past lungs and blades.
Then barren days of white paper,
where longing and I cuddle like lovers,
wishing to go pristine again,
when love was not abrasive, yet sober.

The Want that Wants to Be Wanted

The untended touch
of a long-lost mother
to be invited.

The fat bitten plum
in the son's palm
to be praised.

The tall grass
hiding familiar footsteps
to be remembered.

The empty rooms
of your craving eyes
to be filled.

The searing heart
hammering at the ceiling
to be heard.

The memories
encased in grief
to be forgotten.

The pain of the dry ink
on the paper
to be undone.

The right of the flesh
to a voice of its own
to be granted.

Fugato

I had a birthday yesterday.
Walked the street grateful for
the drizzle and the garbage man,
smiling at some ghost that
strode by my side. A livelier gait.
I had craved salt all day long,
gnawed on puffs and crackers
from the vending machine.
Outside, March failed to unfold.
At home, there is half a pink cake
in the fridge. I started eating it
two days ago, out of spite. This year
time feels too odd to bear.
Last night, I buried my face
under layers of anti-aging cream.
Woke up cranky. In the mirror,
an oily foreign face. That
of grandma Jeni, last Christmas,
sunk in a too big chair, deaf
of both ears, glossy eyes measuring
the commotion. You leaving earlier
to catch the 10:30 Mineola to Jamaica.
I stood in the corner of the room,
nibbling the Florentine quiche
hoping not to smile on green teeth,
and for some reason, couldn't stop.
Somewhere, a cat whimpered like a baby.
Wanted to sit with you on the fire escape
stairs and feed her crumbles from my plate.
Oversalted pieces of eggy spinach.
Between us, a sugar cube of stillness.

Excavation

There is a woman made to look like a mess,
fragmented into instances of domesticity,
smelling like *zacuscă* and wormwood soap
nibbling on homemade bread,
deriving small pleasures from the routine and because of it.
This version of home
is full of legends and false gods, slaying her soul into nothingness.

One grandmother calls her a pain in her bones.
She smiles, kneading a sudden tightness in her left shoulder.
She wipes the old woman's arms
and tries to remember a time when she could fit
the hollow of their embrace.
Outside, the night feels like a well.

She moves in sight, unseen,
a braided scent of moth balls
along the familiar walls,
the moody rhythms of the house,
vibrating.

She's more watchable these days.
Indulged into her cravings,
she bakes her uneasy heart
into different pie flavors.

Late at night, she gazes
into the face of her two babies,
weaving valiant dreams.

On TV, some sepia-toned David Lynch
hallucinating doppelganger fills the room,
enlarging the doubts:

she still dreams
she is a poet
trapped inside a woman's body.

Sasha, 13,

still believes
in things with feathers,
dreams and blue tilts,
nesting memories of lizards,
the abundant touch of lost humans,
mismatched skull earrings,
the call of the lavender
field painting down the hallway,
fragmentation of speech,
Te ube! before going to bed,
dark Netflix heroes that grin
before dashing into the night,
horizontal smiles
on Nutella-smeared toast,
reknitting the day and its splendors,
and everything that is logo hoodies.
At night, asleep under her netted bed,
I watch her long eyelashes,
and forget to breathe.

The View from Here

is a woman who says
she does not allow herself
to sink or cry.
She has said good-bye
so many times,
she has turned it into
an art. The art of fading
into the surface
of her delicious mind
thriving on poems,
loving from a distance,
teaching composition,
taking the LIRR to Manhattan,
OCD-ing at peak hours,
reading and wondering
at other people's tricks
of living in mundane bliss.

I get to meet the woman
quite often. Even share coffee
or a Skinny Girl toffee,
got used to her thick accent
and have come to recognize
her shielded way of carrying
herself and conversations.
I wish I could tell her
loss is a way of knowing.
It comes in choking waves
and alters the taste of food
and the length of days,

might even make one forget
about the living.
If only she stopped worrying
about the height from which
she might fall,

we could take a stroll
down Jericho Avenue,
she could wear her red boots,
taste her own fear of being,
and call it a day.
I could offer to switch places
for a moment,
bear the burden of the day
and give her room to breathe.
Yet, she continues to speak
to something inside her
that longs to be named.
There is grief she carries
for her own living self
and the vague unrest
of her wandering bones.

Displacement

My friend Juan tells me
my accent gets thicker
when my mind wanders off
and I speak of familiar food,
my people or music.
Romanian words are nostalgic and ripen.
My longing spirals down
this invisible burrow like the one
my guinea pigs dug in the garden one night.
When I open my eyes, music fades
and I am back in my other life,
where there is a constant desire
for less flesh.

I am comfortably invisible here,
where everything is a shard of a great promise
and I've learned to live in halves.
New York is a city of disappearance,
a honeycomb of human mirrors,
air filled with calls going unanswered,
traffic gods favoring honking metal
to warm-bloodied walking flames.
When I roam its streets, coiling and uncoiling,
I try to remember from the other life
and its flavor fuels my steps.
I am caught in between, hungry for small things
whose names belong to me alone.

The Strings of Demi-Gods

In *Râmnicu Vâlcea*, Romania,
the myth about the woman's rib lives on.

My father scolds me for raising
a daughter who shaves her nape,
my grandmothers tell me to be good
every time I travel.
That husband of yours is a treasure.

My brother lights a candle
for my wandering womanly heart
every Sunday, then puts on
his acting hat, rehearsing for hours.

My son tells me I need to ask
for permission because every house
has a man, every realm has a king.
I kiss his long lashes
and promise him a world
of different rules.

An aunt comes for coffee
and whispers she knows
the love spell of binding.
I have already given myself.
To another?

I wish I could tell her
that words own me more
than love, in a greedy, ruthless
way, as no man ever
began to understand.

The flesh has learned to bear
the massive burden of the heart,
the blankets of domestic life
and the strings of demi-gods.

In Râmnicu Vâlcea, Romania,
I am a woman of my own ribs,
all 12 pairs made of word bones.

To this day,

loss weighs on my heart
like a tender bruise of light
the dregs of its architecture
still teaching me to love details—
the oyster silences, the IV drip nights,
the fading of the heart, the sweet morphine,
the overlooked everyday conundrums
we shared around the kitchen table
covered in flowery oilcloth,
braids of white garlic and dried chili,
twigs of thyme and brown laurel
spicing and feasting the roofs of our mouths,
the crumbles of the day or the untended bones.

Keeping Things Whole

Today feels like a Sunday,
a soft bracket in the tumult of the week.
I am wearing my mother's face,

a beautiful plate cracked in half,
one hand on the humming dishwater,
the other feeling my mother wound.

The muffled thumping inside the ribs
hits the pane of the laced window,
and I close my eyes to blind the echo.

Soon, there will be breath blooming around,
and face, plates and ghost bird
will gain texture, a standing presence.

A Stranger's Doing

When I come home,
my English sticks to everything.
My son watches me in silence,
uncertain of my restlessness.
Grandma wants to know if I have a cold
and promises to make me a garlic sauce
to wash away the raspy voice,
her eyes a smoldering fire.
My gait, an appendage to the memory.

When I return to NY, on the Mineola track,
an older gentleman calls me Latina.
One girl from Bridges believes
Romania is a third world country,
then adds, I clean up nicely.
I later send her a YouTube video
with the greenest,
tallest mountains she's ever seen.
Home, she smiles. *My Lebanon.*

In my mouth, my native language
turns strange, a stranger's doing.
Home has become elastic, a spare mouth,
the body caught in the burden of stifling days,
its inked veins brimming of contradictions.
The world's roof reeks of fresh poetry,
I take shelter in its lines, a tremble
in its voracious filament. It lights up my darkness.

Snapshot

Through the thin venetian blinds,
over the tall patch of sky,
birds erupt like rash.
Their winged, passing throb
puzzles the air, my throat full
of cascading feelings.
One grandma made it
through the night, the other one
remembered to take her pills,
one kid, softly curled on the couch,
ruining teeth on Cadbury buttons,
another getting lost in my clothes.
You dangle your left slipper,
sipping cold coffee and watching
worries peel in the air.
Days like these foaming
with little celebrations.

Dear NY,

I'm back to my Easter European small town
where I'm trying to understand
how we all become strangers
in the most familiar stretch of skin.

Permanence is but a fistful of pine needles
in the condensation of a train window
where I am caught in the vacant space between drops.

Across an ocean and two seas,
there's a world where I thought
I could live without longing,
yet the pungent scent
of your gutted and deboned streets,
the whisper of thawing bodies,
and the geared clockworks of your blood
keep custody of my heart.

Half-drunk with your distanced gifts,
I lean my head against the back seat of the taxi,
Oriental music filling the narrow space,
and I ask the driver to take me nowhere in particular,
just spin around, until my heart unlearns to remember.

How fat with love I was, trying to feign sleep
on the LIRR off-peak train, back from poetry readings,
just to keep words bursting out of my chest like birds.
How I used to live in each artery of ink
that ran your speckled body,
and made sense of my loneliness and giant dreams.

Process of Detachment

I expect my son will let go of me when he's five.
I will go back to just being Clara.
So ready to unspool from the erupting teeth,
the needy eyes, the extra hugs, the sticky fingers
and slip back into my old unprompted self.
The one who walked hard and spoke loudly,
flirted, craving to feel armies of ionized butterflies
prickle her backbone and warm her cheeks.
Of course, my body will stay proof of my shortcomings,
the twitching finger of the world pointing
at the curves, folds, scars. Little aware of the invisible.
The dreams of the young woman sipping
her latte at the corner of Franklyn and 7th Street,
a book of Dorianne Laux poems in her hand,
the nimble autumn breeze brushing her naked ankles.
The sleep-deprived, heavy breathing, nursing mom
who could not take her eyes off of the translucent skin
of the stubborn eyelids that took two weeks to open.
In between, there is a poet who craves the particulars
of other people's frailties so she could match her own,
nib and heart probing the wound that lurks behind ecstasy.

The Body's Questions

What is the name
for the mother who isn't?

What is the meaning for bread
that rises in a house that falls,
no one to bless its miracle?

What is the name for the ghost
that grows under cracked flesh?

What is the name for peeling
at the corner of wallpaper,
only to find more of yourself?

What is the name for ink
bruising paper?

What is the name for berries
heavy with summer
and no mouth to eat them?

What is the name for a leaf
carried down a stream?

What is the name of a heart
draining like sands
from a dry foot?

What is the name of the cushion
reshaping the vacant couch?

What is the name for a woman
who leaves her children
for poems?

NOTES:

Portocale is the Romanian word for orange.

Ţuică is homemade plum brandy.

Zacuscă is a Romanian homemade spread made of roasted eggplants, onions, beans and tomatoes sauce.

Râmnicu Vâlcea is a small town in Romania.

About the Author

CLARA BURGHELEA is a Romanian-born poet and translator. She received her MFA in Poetry from Adelphi University. Recipient of the Robert Muroff Poetry Award, her poems and translations appeared in Ambit, HeadStuff, Waxwing and elsewhere. She reads for various magazines and is the current Poetry Editor of *The Blue Nib*.

For the full Dos Madres Press catalog:
www.dosmadres.com